BRANDYWINE PUBLIC SCHOOLS
Elementary Library
2428 S. 13th Street
Niles, MI 49120

D1803720

THE CONTINUING REVOLUTION

Read for accuracy by

Series Consultant
David McDonald
Professor of History
University of Wisconsin—Madison

Copyright © 1989 Raintree Publishers Limited Partnership

All rights reserved. No portion of this book may be reproduced or utilized in any form or by any means, electronic or mechanical, including photocopying, recording, or by any information storage and retrieval system, without permission in writing from the Publishers. Inquiries should be addressed to Raintree Publishers, 310 West Wisconsin Avenue, Milwaukee, Wisconsin 53203.

Library of Congress Number: 89-3688

1 2 3 4 5 6 7 8 9   94 93 92 91 90 89

Library of Congress Cataloging-in-Publication Data

Clark, James I.
  The continuing revolution / James I. Clark.
  (Portrait of the Soviet Union)
  Includes index.
  Summary: Describes the successful Communist takeover of Russia, the establishment of the Soviet Union, and the contributions of subsequent regimes, with particular attention given to foreign relations after World War II.
  1. Soviet Union—History—1917- —Juvenile literature. 2. Soviet Union—Foreign relations—1945- —Juvenile literature. [1. Soviet Union—History—1917. 2. Soviet Union—Foreign relations—1945-]
  I. Title. II. Series: Clark, James I. Portrait of the Soviet Union.
DK266.C56   1989   947.084—dc19   89-3688
  ISBN 0-8172-3357-1 (hardcover)
  ISBN 0-8172-3367-9 (softcover)

Cover Photo: TBS/Reagan

THE CONTINUING REVOLUTION

James I. Clark

RAINTREE PUBLISHERS
Milwaukee

CONTENTS

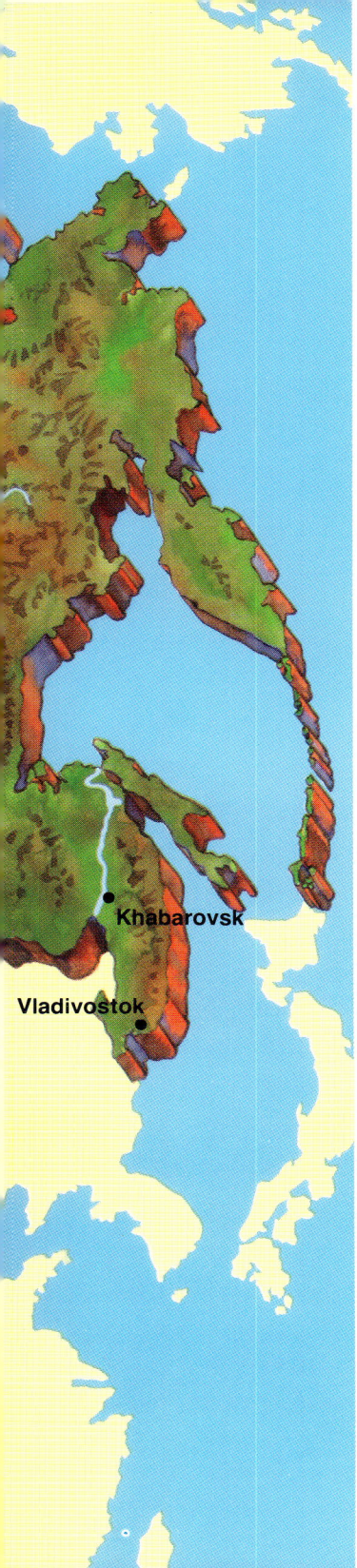

Introduction	**6**
Maker of Revolution	**8**
The Second Revolution	**10**
Communists in Control	**12**
Government and Party	**14**
The Soviet Union Under Lenin	**17**
Man of Steel	**18**
Five-Year Plans and Purges	**22**
The Great Patriotic War	**25**
The Cold War	**29**
New Leaders and Better Relations	**32**
The Soviet Union Under Brezhnev	**35**
A Nice Smile, but Teeth of Steel	**37**
Glasnost	**38**
Perestroika	**40**
The Soviet Union and Other Countries	**44**
A Chronology of the Soviet Union	**46**
Map of Soviet Republics	**47**
Index	**48**

INTRODUCTION

Nineteen-seventeen began as a grim year for Russians. World War I had gone badly, bringing defeats by German armies and leaving millions of Russian soldiers dead, wounded, or captured. Food shortages in cities had brought rioting. People blamed Czar Nicholas II for the way the war had gone. He became an object of hatred. Troubles were everywhere. To many people, to be Russian meant to live in misery.

Then, suddenly, everything changed. In March, the Duma stopped taking orders from the czar. The Duma was a group of elected representatives who were to make laws for Russia. In Petrograd, the capital of Russia, soldiers and officers sent to put down riots refused to obey orders. They joined the rioters. Finally, with both the Duma and the army against him, Nicholas II gave up the throne. That ended three hundred years of rule by his family, the Romanovs. Russia would no longer have a czar.

Grimness now turned to hope. Russia might have a chance for democratic government. For Russians, the hated war might soon end.

A thirty-story monument honors the Soviet victory at Stalingrad during World War II.

Maker of Revolution

Russia had two revolutions in 1917. The first came unexpectedly, in March. The second came after some planning, in November. It ended with the nation under Communist control.

The man who organized Russia's second revolution was Vladimir Ilyich Ulyanov. He is better known by his revolutionary name, Lenin.

Lenin was born on April 22, 1870, in the village of Simbirsk, on the Volga River. The village is now called Ulyanovsk. His father was a schoolteacher. His mother was the daughter of a doctor, and she had had a good education. Lenin had two brothers and three sisters. He was especially fond of his older brother, Alexander.

As a youth, Lenin liked to swim, fish, hike, and play chess. He also liked to read, and he did very well in his studies at school.

Lenin's father died when he was sixteen, in 1886. The next year his brother Alexander was arrested for taking part in a plot to kill the czar, Alexander III. Alexander Ulyanov was hanged.

That same year Lenin began studies at a university. He was

expelled for taking part in a student demonstration for more freedom there. He moved to another university, where he studied to be a lawyer. He also studied revolution. Thus, Lenin became a part of the broader revolutionary tradition that had its roots in the 1820s. Lenin had begun these studies be-

fore his brother had been arrested and hanged. After that, he had become even more determined to work for change in Russia.

In the capital of Russia, Lenin

At right: *Vladimir Ilych Ulyanov, who took the revolutionary name Lenin. Lenin's mummified body is on view to visitors at Moscow's Red Square (above).*

Above: *the faces of communism's founders still preside over everyday Soviet life.*

joined a revolutionary group and soon became its leader. The police arrested him and sent him to Siberia. After three years, Lenin received police permission to leave Russia. He lived at various times in Germany, England, Sweden, and Switzerland. He spent much of his time writing pamphlets and newspaper articles in favor of revolution in Russia. He also kept in touch with fellow revolutionaries there.

The Second Revolution

Lenin was in Switzerland when revolution came to Russia in March 1917. He immediately made plans to return home to take charge, and Germany would help him. German leaders knew that Lenin wanted Russia out of the war. If that happened, Germany then could give all its attention to fighting England and France, countries that were on Russia's side. Lenin promised that if he achieved power in Russia, that nation would indeed leave the war, so the Germans put Lenin and about thirty of his followers on a train. The train took them to Petrograd.

In that city and in others, workers had formed councils called Soviets. The Soviet of Workers' and Soldiers' Deputies in Petrograd shared power with the government. Lenin demanded "all power to the Soviets." He also called for an end to Russia's participation in the war. He also demanded that the national government take over land, factories, and other things used to produce goods people needed, along with banks, railroads, and telephone and telegraph companies.

The Russian government was controlled by a number of political parties. Many of them believed in government ownership, but many believed that change should come gradually and in a democratic way. Some groups wanted Russia to stay in the war. That, they said, was a matter of national honor, and Germany might eventually lose. If so, Russia might gain land it wanted.

Lenin's followers, called Bolsheviks, tried to seize control of the government. They failed, and Lenin fled to Finland.

The government under the Mensheviks, however, satisfied no one. Peasants wanted land. People in cities wanted food and fuel. Nearly everyone wanted Russia out of the war. But the government did not meet these demands.

Lenin arrived to find a Russia where power was divided between Workers' Soviets and a weak provisional government. Lenin called for the transfer of all power to the Soviets.

Lenin uses a truckbed as a platform from which to address a crowd during the November Revolution.

Communists in Control

Early in November 1917, Lenin returned to Petrograd. He urged his followers to again move to seize power. "The government is wavering," he said. "It must be given the finishing blow at all costs. To delay action will be fatal." Lenin was right. The weak government disappeared overnight as Bolsheviks, aided by some sailors and soldiers, took over important buildings and streets. Soon all Petrograd was theirs, and they took over Moscow as well. They promised "bread, peace, and land."

Now in control, the Bolsheviks changed their name to the Russian Communist Party. As head of the government and the party, Lenin became dictator.

Peace came early the following

year. The new Russian government made a treaty with Germany. Fighting would stop, but Russia had to agree to give up land it controlled in Poland, Finland, and along the Baltic Sea, as well as the Russian region called the Ukraine.

The war ended in 1918. Germany was defeated, in great part because of help from the United States, which had entered the war against Germany the year before. Russia now gained back some of the land it had agreed to give up. It lost only land in Poland and along the Baltic Sea, which became the nations of Lithuania, Latvia, and Estonia, and land in Finland.

Communists did not have power in all of Russia, and they faced a long and bloody civil war to gain it. Those who opposed the Communists themselves were called Reds. During the civil war, battles were fought throughout Russia.

The leaders of several nations feared that Communist revolution might spread outside of Russia, which is what Lenin wanted to happen. So England, France, Japan, Poland, and the United States sent soldiers to Russia to fight the Red army.

Soon after taking over the government, the Communists made the former Czar Nicholas II and his family prisoners. During the civil war, the Communists feared that the Whites might recapture the family, and make Nicholas II czar once again. They had Nicholas, his wife Alexandra, and their five children shot to death.

The civil war lasted nearly four years. In the end, the Red army won. Communists now set up a secret police force to seek out and

Below: *Red Guards stand outside the cabinet of Lenin and his revolutionary advisors.*

destroy anyone who opposed the party. Moscow became the nation's capital once again. In 1924, the city of Petrograd became Leningrad, and Russia became the Union of Soviet Socialist Republics. In Russian, it is Soyuz Sovetskikh Sotsialisticheskikh Respublik. The initials are S.S.S.R.

Soviet means "council." *Socialist* refers to government ownership of everything in the name of the people. *Republics* means that each of the areas into which the nation is divided has its own government. The republics also form a *union* under the government of the nation.

In most republics, the majority of the people belong to one national or ethnic group. Armenians are in the majority in the Armenian Republic, for example. Most of the people in the Kazakh Republic are Kazaks.

Government and Party

The Communist party controlled the government that was set up in the Soviet Union, and that remains the case today.

One part of the government is the Congress of People's Deputies, made up of 2,250 members. Of these, 1,500 are elected from the fifteen republics and territories within them. The remaining 750 are elected from such organizations as the Communist party, labor unions, and youth groups. The Congress of People's Deputies meets once a year to decide on overall economic and social policy.

Laws are made by the Supreme Soviet, which has 400 to 450 members elected by the Congress of People's Deputies. The Supreme Soviet meets twice a year for two or three months at a time. It elects a Presidum, or steering committee, made up of representatives of the fifteen republics, along with others, to make decisions between sessions.

The Congress of People's Deputies also elects the president, who can have only two five-year terms. The president has a hand in making laws and guides relations with other nations, defense programs, and the Presidium of the Supreme Soviet.

Finally, there is a Council of Ministers. Its members are responsible for such things as trade with other countries, education, and public health. The chairman of

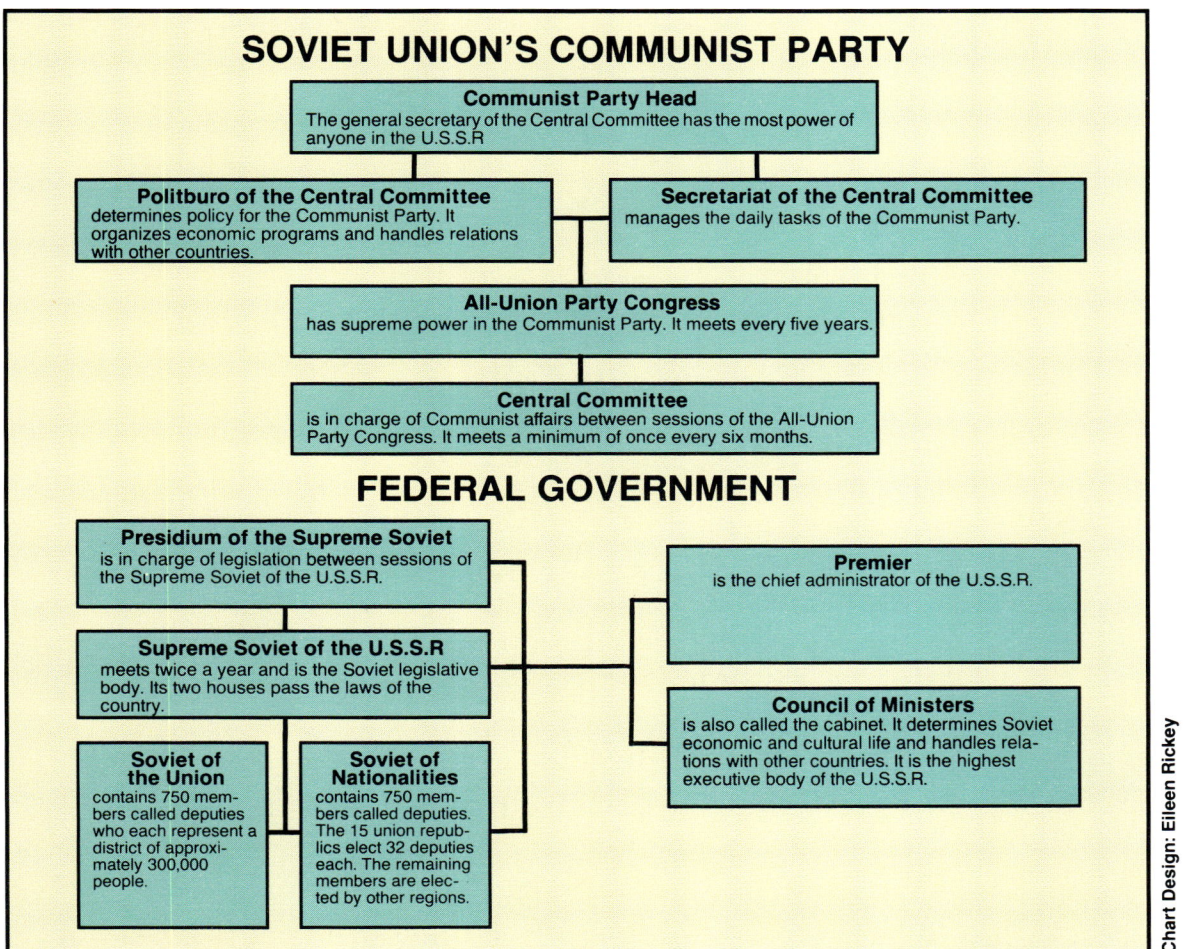

the council is called the premier, or prime minister.

Nearly all members of government in the Soviet Union belong to the Communist party, which has about seventeen million members in the entire nation. To join the party, a person must be eighteen years old. He or she must be recommended by three persons who have been party members for at least five years. They must have known the person wishing to join for at least one year. The person must then wait a year before he or she is permitted to join.

There are party organizations in factories, villages, on collective farms, in the army, navy, and air force, and in colleges and univer-

sities. There is also a party organization in each republic.

Party organizations elect the All-Union party Congress. It is made up of five thousand members. The Congress, in turn, elects the Central Committee of 560 members. That group chooses members of the Politburo, which is headed by the general secretary. The Politburo meets in secret, and it is the most powerful group in the Soviet Union.

Citizens elect members of both republic and national soviets. However, the Communist party decides who the candidates will be, and a voter can vote for those candidates or not vote at all. The Supreme Soviet makes laws for the nation, but leaders of the Communist party decide which laws will be made. The same is true of laws made in the republics.

The Soviet Union Under Lenin

Once in power, with Lenin in charge, the Soviet government took over land, banks, mines, and factories. Hundreds of thousands of engineers, factory managers, and other skilled workers left the country. As a result, many factories closed, and workers were out of jobs. They had no money to buy food. The government ordered farmers to turn over grain and vegetables to feed workers in cities. Farmers were not paid for their crops, and they fought back by raising only enough to feed themselves.

The government backed away. It gave land to peasants and allowed them to sell their crops for cash. The government kept banks and large factories but returned many small factories to their owners. As a result, living conditions in the Soviet Union improved.

Under Lenin, the Soviet government also took over land owned by the Russian Orthodox Church, and it closed churches. Religious groups, Communists said, had always taken the side of the rulers and wealthy people against the common people. Religion was to have no place in the Soviet Union. In schools, young people would be taught that there is no God.

Lenin suffered a stroke in 1922. Then he had a second and a third. He died on January 21, 1924. The

Left: *St. Isaac's Cathedral in Leningrad. After the revolution forbid its use as a place of worship, the church was made a state museum.*

body of the father of Russian communism was placed in an airtight glass case in a tomb in Moscow's Red Square. The tomb became the Soviet Union's most important monument.

Man of Steel

The death of Lenin left the Soviet Union and the Communist party without a leader. Many people expected leadership to go to Leon Trotsky. He had worked closely with Lenin in the revolution, and he had organized and led the Red Army to fight the civil war. But Trotsky would not be the new Soviet leader. It would be a man named Josif Vissarionovich Djugashvili. Like Lenin and others, he too had a revolutionary name. It was Stalin. In Russian, *stalin* means "man of steel," and that is just what Josif Vissarionovich Djugashvili proved to be.

Right: *crowds line up to view the body of Lenin at his mausoleum in Red Square. An undisclosed embalming process has kept the Soviet leader's remains perfectly preserved since his death in 1924.*

Left: *Joseph Stalin is shown against the background of his native Georgia (above). Stalin proved to be a ruthless leader who concentrated all power in his own hands.*

Joseph Stalin was born on December 21, 1879 in the village of Gori, in what is now the Republic of Georgia. As a child, he did not have a happy life. The family lived in a shack. Stalin's father was a poor shoemaker and a

drunkard. He often beat his son. Stalin's mother washed other people's clothing to earn money to help the family survive. Stalin had smallpox when he was six or seven years old. This left his face badly scarred. His three siblings died shortly after they were born.

Stalin's mother managed to send him to school, and he did well in his studies. At age fourteen, he decided to become a priest in the Russian Orthodox Church. While studying to be a priest, Stalin also studied revolution. By the time he was twenty-one, he was a revolutionary himself.

That got him into trouble with the police. Stalin was arrested and put in prison. Then he was sent to Siberia. He escaped from there, and after he returned, he joined the Bolsheviks. During the next several years, Stalin was in and out of prison. Although he took part in the revolution, he was not nearly so important to it as Lenin, Trotsky, and others.

After the civil war, Lenin made Stalin general secretary of the Communist party. This fit Stalin's plans well. He now would know everything about the party's business. He could give jobs in the party to people who would be loyal to him.

Within a few years after Lenin died, Stalin got rid of anyone in the party who might oppose him. He now became chief leader of the party and the nation. Joseph Stalin became dictator.

Above: *Stalin's Five-Year Plans gave many rural areas their first electric power.*

Five-Year Plans and Purges

Stalin set up the first of many Five-Year Plans in 1928. One part of it aimed to increase the output of oil, iron and steel, and electrical power, and to build more factories. Factories produced trucks, tractors and other farm machinery, railroad cars and locomotives, and other heavy goods. They did not produce many radios, refrigerators, or automobiles or as much clothing or other things as people wanted to buy.

Another part of the Five-Year Plan aimed to increase the supply of food. To do this, the government took land from farmers. It set up huge farms. Some became state farms, and others became collectives. Farmers would raise crops for the government. In return, they would be paid wages, just like factory workers.

Farmers of the Soviet Union fought the idea of collectives. Many refused to work for the government. They grew only enough food for themselves. They killed their cows, hogs, and horses so the government could not take them. The government then used force. It killed hundreds of thousands of farmers and shipped about three million off to Siberia. There they worked as prisoners in mines and in forests.

Five-Year Plans also paid attention to education. Many schools were built, and going to school became a part of nearly every young person's life. Eventually, 99 percent of Soviet citizens could read and write. Hospitals were built, and the number of doctors and nurses increased.

Soviet citizens, however, enjoyed little freedom, as Americans and others understood the word. The government decided where people would work and how much they would be paid. Newspapers printed what the government told them to print. The government would allow only certain books and magazines to be published. Scientists had no freedom to try experiments they wished or to explore new ideas. No one enjoyed freedom of speech, or even of thought. Stalin's secret police were everywhere. A person who said anything against the government would have a one-way ticket to Siberia. Soviet citizens could not travel outside their

The new Soviet state moved sometimes unevenly in its advance into the twentieth century. A factory worker listens to a modern radio apparatus amid this otherwise rustic setting.

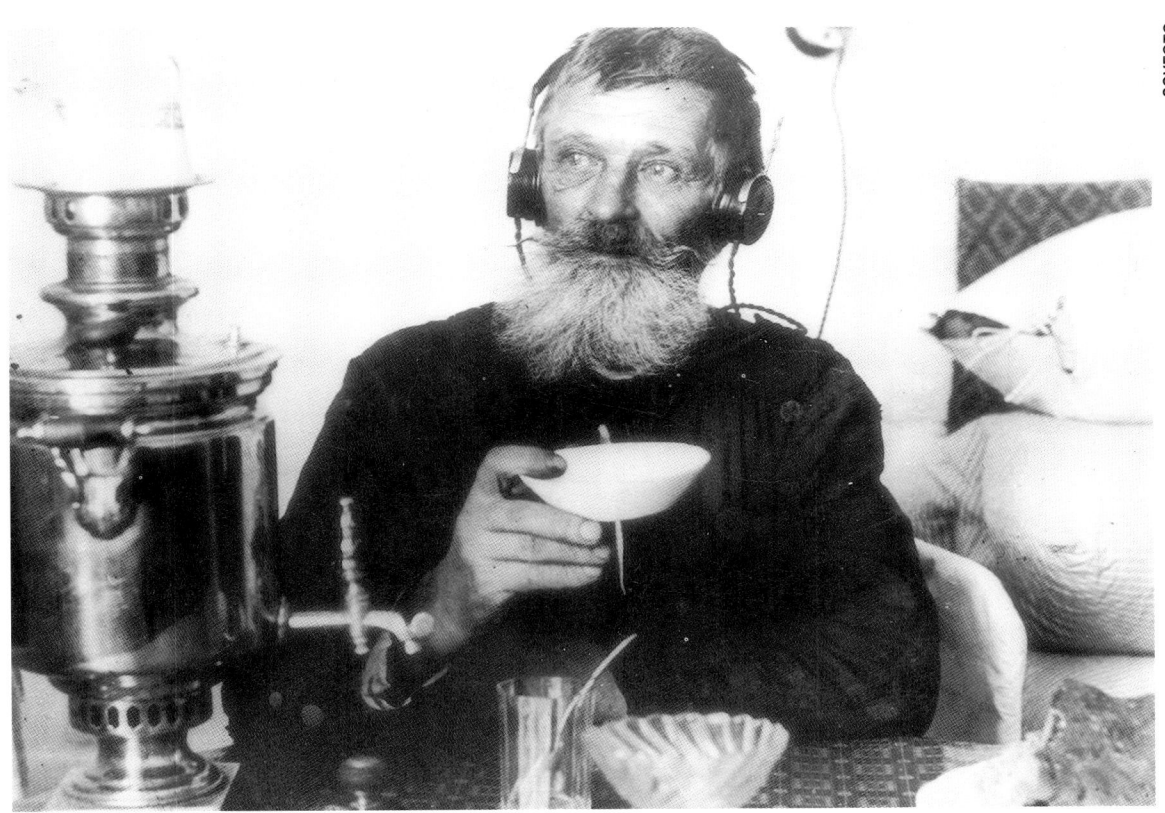

country without government permission, and that was hard to get.

During all their history, Russians had never enjoyed individual liberties. In the past, the czar's word had been law. Now it was the Communist party's word.

Soviet citizens did have certain rights, however. They had the right to a job, a place to live, an education, and health care. They were free from worry about being out of work and without an income. The government paid workers' wages and provided places to live at low cost. It also kept food prices low. Citizens did not need to worry about paying doctor and hospital bills. The government paid them. From the Communist point of view, the rights Soviet citizens enjoyed were more important than the rights of freedom of speech, thought, and movement.

Stalin still had enemies. Some of them were real. Some of them were imagined. To get rid of all of them he began a purge, that is, an elimination. Stalin purged those he considered enemies from the Communist party, the Red Army, and other organizations. Altogether, about eight million people were killed. Another ten million were sent to prison or to labor camps in

The major shaping experience of Soviet history was the nation's costly war with Hitler. Since the war, the U.S.S.R has maintained a large army to protect itself from further invasions. Recruits drawn from the many republics serve together.

Siberia.

The Great Patriotic War

The Soviet Union had just begun its third Five-Year Plan when war broke out again in Europe.

Germany had been defeated in World War I. It began to become a powerful nation again in the 1930s under the dictator Adolf Hitler. Hitler built up Germany's army and navy. He planned to use that nation's armed might to conquer all of Europe.

Ignoring his nonaggression pact with Stalin, Hitler attacked the U.S.S.R. in June, 1941.

First Germany took over the nearby nation of Austria. Then it took over Czechoslovakia. Next Hitler demanded that Poland give up land to Germany. The government of Poland refused, and the governments of England and France backed it up. Hitler then made an agreement of friendship with Stalin. Finally, in September 1939, he sent his armies into Poland, and England and France declared war on Germany. The Soviet Union did nothing to help Poland, and Germany quickly conquered that nation. Germany and Russia divided Poland between them.

The Soviet Union then fought a war with Finland and took land from that nation. Next it took over Lithuania, Estonia, and Latvia. Those nations became republics within the U.S.S.R. The Soviet Union also took Bessarabia from Rumania and made it the Republic of Moldavia.

Within a year and a half after defeating Poland, Germany conquered France and several other European nations. Soon England was left to fight Hitler alone. Hitler now tore up his treaty of friendship with Stalin. In a surprise attack, his armies invaded the Soviet Union.

Hitler had nearly won six months after war with the Soviet Union began. In the first two weeks, Russia lost more than a million soldiers and thousands of tanks and planes. German armies moved deeply into the Soviet Union, coming close to Moscow and Leningrad. The Germans bombed and shelled Leningrad, keeping its people trapped for nine hundred

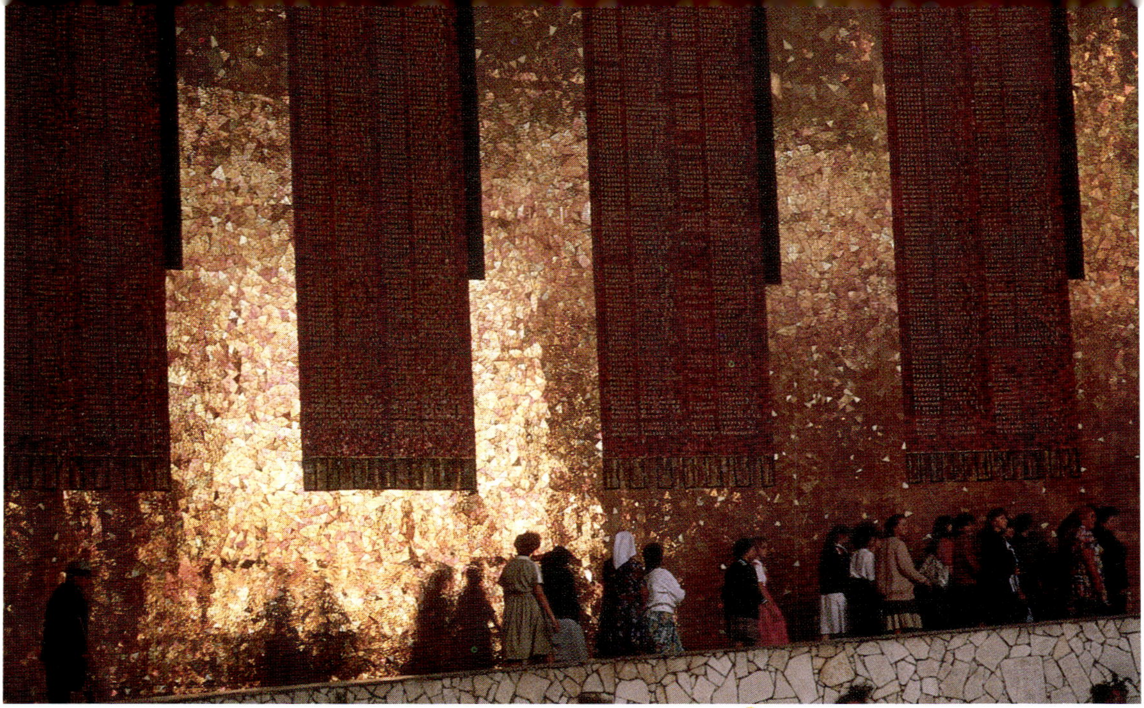

TBS/Reagan

The Great Patriotic War remains a living memory for the Soviet people. Shown on this page are monuments honoring the war dead in Leningrad cemeteries.

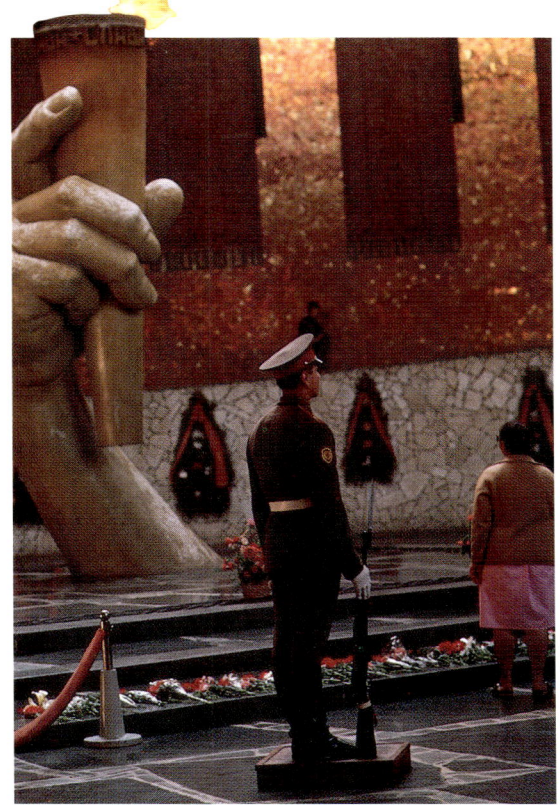

days. They ate insects and rats and chewed on leather and drank soup made from glue to try to stay alive. Hundreds of thousands starved to death.

In a radio broadcast Stalin said: "The Red Army and Navy and the whole Soviet people must fight for every inch of Soviet soil, fight to the last drop of our blood for our towns and villages." A Russian writer said: "We must not say, 'Good morning' or 'Good night.' In the morning we must say, 'Kill the Germans,' and at night we must

TBS/Reagan

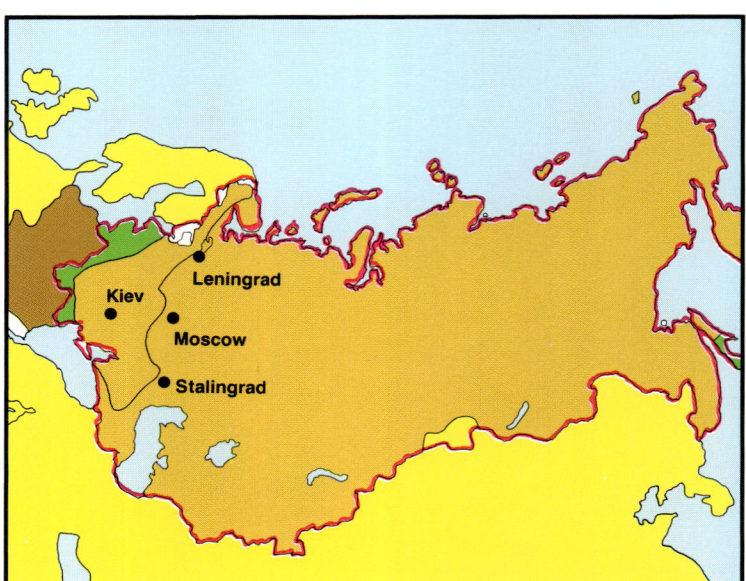

say, 'Kill the Germans.' We want to live and in order to live, we must kill Germans."

Final defeat for the Germans in Russia began with the Battle of Stalingrad, on the Volga River, south and east of Moscow. The battle was the turning point of the war. It raged for months. Soldiers fought hand to hand, street by street, building by building. At last, the German troops surrendered. Three hundred thousand had been killed, wounded, or captured. After Stalingrad, the Red Army began to roll the Germans back, pushing them toward their homeland.

In the meantime, Japan attacked the United States in the Pacific, and World War II came to America. Germany now declared war on the United States. The United States had helped the Soviets with war materials, and it now stepped up that aid. American armies, along with English and French soldiers, attacked Germany from the west. United States and Russian soldiers met in Germany, and the Soviets took over that nation's capital, Berlin. The war in Europe ended in May 1945.

In Russia, the war is called The Great Patriotic War. It left twenty-one million Soviet soldiers and civilians dead. It ruined great areas of the nation. But Germany had been defeated, and the Soviet Union was now the strongest nation in Europe.

The Cold War

During World War II, the Soviet Union had fought alongside the United States and England against Germany. Now the Soviet Union would no longer cooperate. Joseph Stalin did not trust such countries as the United States and England, especially the United States. Americans were strongly against communism, and Stalin believed that the United States planned to destroy his government. The United States and other nations did not trust Stalin, especially after what happened in central and eastern Europe.

Many people expected that after World War II, countries Germany had conquered there would be-

The veterans who helped drive the Nazi invaders from Soviet soil are still reverend heroes in the U.S.S.R. Below: a Ukrainian farmer displays a chestful of decorations.

come democracies. Joseph Stalin, however, had other plans. More than once, armies from the west had marched into Russia. Stalin would prevent this from happening again by having governments he could depend on along Russia's western border. As a result, often with aid from the Red Army, those countries got Communist governments. There were no free elections. Those nations were Poland, Hungary, Romania, Bulgaria, Czechoslovakia, Yugoslavia, and Albania. In addition, the Soviet Union took over the eastern part of Germany. That area became East Germany, also under a Communist government.

The United States worked to prevent the spread of communism by giving billions of dollars to several European countries. This helped them rebuild after the war

A monument in Volgograd shows Mother Russia mourning her lost children . . . the twenty million Soviet citizens killed during World War II. Soviets vow never to repeat such a tragedy.

and made jobs for millions of workers. The United States also helped European countries build up their armies, navies, and air forces. In Europe, communism did not spread beyond those nations near the Soviet Union.

During World War II, the United States developed a nuclear bomb. It used the bomb twice on Japan. Then, soon after the war ended, the Soviet Union—through espionage—also developed a nuclear bomb. Now, in the midst of poor relations between the United States and Russia, people came to fear nuclear war between the two nations. That would could destroy most of the world.

This time of great distrust between the Soviet Union and other countries was called the Cold War. It went on for many years.

The Soviet Union itself became a closed nation. It did not welcome visitors from other countries. Whatever freedom its citizens had had during the war disappeared. Workers could not change jobs without permission. More land was put into collective farms. The secret police were active, and many people were sent to prison or to Siberia.

Human casualties of the Great Patriotic War are still visible. Above: two veterans remember at Leningrad's War Memorial.

Jews had an especially hard time under Stalin. They were not allowed to have government jobs. They had difficulty getting into colleges and universities. They could not have their own newspapers. They could not practice their religion freely.

Such treatment was nothing new to Russian Jews. They had been persecuted, killed, and sent to Siberia under the czars. In the past, though, Jews could leave Russia, and some two million came to the United States. Now many Jews wished to leave Russia for the new nation of Israel. The government allowed scarcely any to go.

During a trip to the United States, Khrushchev visits the Coon Rapids, Iowa, farm of Garst Seed Company owner Roswell Garst.

New Leaders and Better Relations

Stalin died on March 5, 1953. For the next five years, several different leaders ruled Russia. Then Nikita Khrushchev, who had been general secretary of the Communist party, also became premier—that is, head of government.

Under Khrushchev, Soviet society grew more open. The Soviet name for this period was "the thaw." Scientists, writers, and painters were allowed greater freedom. Workers had to be on the job just forty hours a week, and they could change jobs if they wished. Relations with other nations, especially with the United States, began to improve.

Khrushchev still believed that communism would eventually win all over the world. But he said that could happen without war. In the meantime, he said, the Soviet Union could have "peaceful coexistence" with non-Communist nations.

Nikita Khrushchev made several journeys outside the Soviet Union. He became the first Russian leader to visit the United States. Khrushchev had talks with President Dwight D. Eisenhower, and he traveled to several places in America, including a farm in Iowa.

There continued to be spots of trouble between the Soviet Union and the United States, though. President Eisenhower was to meet again with Khrushchev, in France. Then the Russians brought down an American spy plane that was taking pictures from high over the Soviet Union. To many Russians, such spying showed that the United States still could not be trusted. Khrushchev called off the meeting with Eisenhower.

A more serious problem came up a few years later. Cuba had be-

Below: *street artists sketch passersby at an outdoor cafe in Kiev. Since the time of Khrushchev, artists have enjoyed greater freedom of expression than previously allowed.*

COUNTRIES WITH COMMUNIST GOVERNMENTS

(indicated in blue)

come a Communist nation, which the Soviet Union aided. It also supplied Cuba with nuclear missiles. This alarmed Americans. Cuba was only 90 miles (145 km) away. Missiles from there could easily hit many American cities.

President John F. Kennedy demanded that Russia remove the missiles from Cuba. For a time, it looked as though the two superpowers would go to war over the question. Then Khrushchev backed down. The missiles were removed.

Khrushchev's action did not set well with other high officials of the Soviet government. Besides, under his leadership, Soviet farms did not produce nearly as much food as the nation needed. Facto-

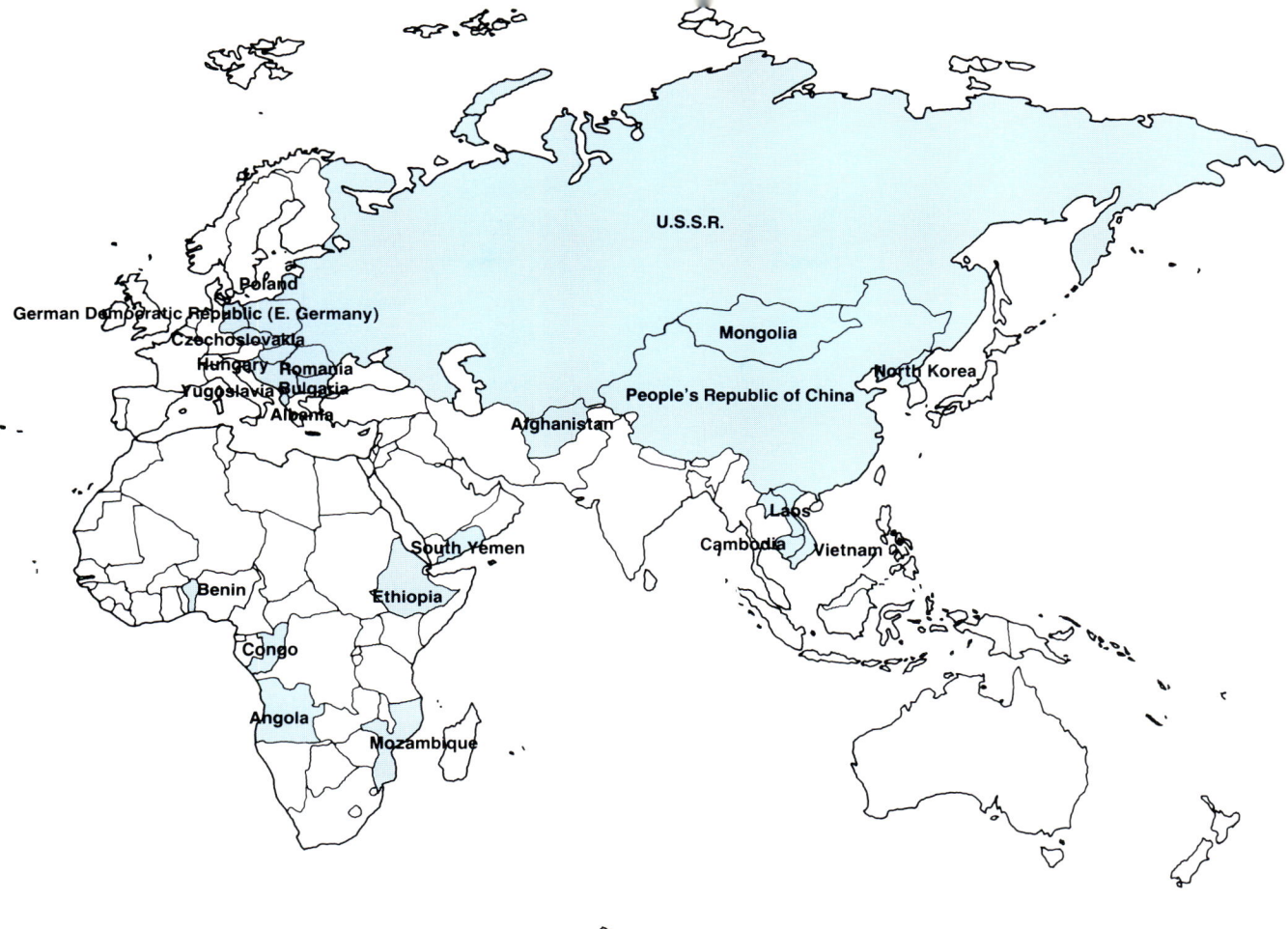

ries did not turn out nearly enough goods people wanted to buy. Those leaders forced Khrushchev to leave office. Leonid I. Brezhnev became general secretary. Later he became premier as well.

The Soviet Union Under Brezhnev

Under Brezhnev, farm and factory production increased. And the Soviet Union continued to have fairly good relations with nations of western Europe and with the United States. Russian trade with other nations increased. Brezhnev met with such American leaders as Presidents Richard M. Nixon and Gerald Ford to discuss problems the United States and the Soviet Union had with each other.

During the 1970s the United States and the U.S.S.R. underwent a process of détente, or easing of tensions. Above: Leonid Brezhnev argues a point with President Nixon.

To Americans, one problem was the lack of human rights in Russia. There was more freedom than under Stalin, but the secret police still kept a close watch, and people were far from entirely free. Americans criticized the Soviet government for that. So did some Soviet citizens. And they landed in prisons or in Siberia.

Americans also wanted the Soviet Union to allow Jews to leave the country if they wished. Finally, over a period of twelve years, the government let about a quarter of a million Jews go.

Relations between the United States and Russia grew worse late in 1979. Russian troops invaded Afghanistan, a small country that borders the Soviet Union on the south. Afghanistan had a Communist government, but it got into trouble when its people revolted against it. Russia aimed to save that government.

The United States protested the invasion. President Jimmy Carter ordered shipments of grain from the United States to Russia be stopped. He would not allow Americans to take part in the 1980 Olympic Games, which were to be held in Moscow. In return, the Soviet Union did not allow its athletes to take part in the 1984 Olympics, which were held in Los Angeles. America sent guns and other weapons to help the rebels in Afghanistan.

Leonid I. Brezhnev died in 1982, and the Soviet Union would now have three leaders in fewer than three years. Yuri V. Andropov took Brezhnev's place. He died in 1984. Konstantin V. Chernenko became Russia's leader. He died thirteen months later. Mikhail Gorbachev became general secretary of the Communist party.

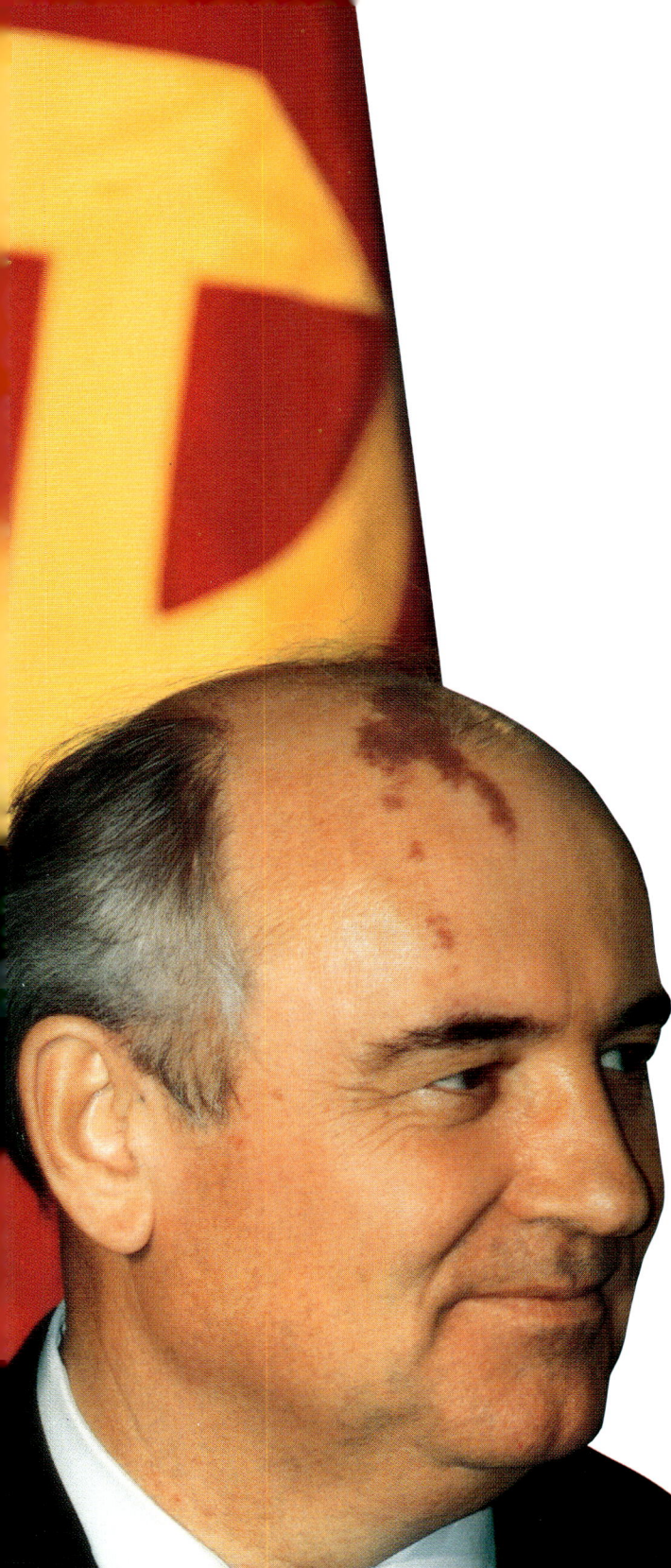

A Nice Smile, but Teeth of Steel

Mikhail Gorbachev was born on March 2, 1931, in the small farming village of Privolnoye, near the city of Stavropol, in southwestern Russia. Both his father and his grandfather had been members of the Communist party.

When he was nineteen, Gorbachev left his village to study law at Moscow State University. He became a member of the Communist party in 1952. Gorbachev had various jobs in government when Brezhnev was general secretary. When Gorbachev became a member of the Politburo, he was the youngest person there. One member said of him: "This man has a nice smile, but he has teeth of steel."

Mikhail Gorbachev would prove to be a leader who listened and who had ideas for change. He was a stern leader who would see that his ideas were carried out.

During his first few months as general secretary, Gorbachev got rid of many elderly members of the government and the party. He

Mikhail Gorbachev's policy of glasnost, or openness, has made this Soviet leader more available to the people than were his predecessors.

UPI/BETTMANN Newsphotos

put younger men in their places. And he set out to get acquainted with the Soviet people.

Gorbachev met people on the streets of Moscow, Leningrad, and other cities. He visited grocery stores, department stores, and factories. One person said that in Leningrad, as Gorbachev was surrounded by eager talkers and listeners, a woman called out:

"You should be closer to the people." Gorbachev replied with a laugh: "How can I get any closer?" He also visited schools, where he went about teaching students to use computers. He visited farms. Everywhere he went, Gorbachev listened to people and explained ideas he had for change in the Soviet Union. He also made sure that television cameras followed him, so that the Soviet people everywhere could learn about his "walkabouts" on the evening news.

Glasnost

Going out to meet and talk with ordinary people was part of Mikhail Gorbachev's idea of *glasnost*, which means "openness." Glasnost also meant that newspapers were more free to print news that was not favorable to the government, and to criticize the government. People were more free to travel in the Soviet Union, and more Soviet citizens were allowed to travel to other countries. Citizens could talk more openly to visitors from foreign nations. They could now obtain and read certain books that had been forbidden in their country. Some people who had not been allowed to speak out or had been put in prison for their ideas were set free. Andrei Sakha-

Glasnost has meant greater freedom for critics of the Soviet government like Andrei Sakharov (below).

rov was an example of this.

Andrei Sakharov was a famous physicist. He had helped develop nuclear weapons for Russia. However, he had become concerned about the lack of human rights in his native land, and he spoke out about this. Sakharov won the Noble Peace Prize for his work for human rights. He also criticized Soviet education and health care. The government did not like what Sakharov had to say. It finally forced him to move from Moscow to the city of Gorgy. The government forbade him to leave there. In 1986, though, Sakharov was allowed to return to Moscow.

Openness went only so far, though. Mikhail Gorbachev finally scolded newspapers for criticizing the government too much. He said they exaggerated Russia's problems. They were turning people against his government and making it harder to bring change to Russia. Newspapers began to quiet down.

In 1986 there was an accident at a nuclear power plant in Chernobyl, near Kiev. About thirty people died, and many others grew ill from radiation sickness. Few people outside of Chernobyl knew

Above: a year after the accident at Chernobyl, children are tested for the effects of radiation.

about the accident because the government said nothing, even though its people and those in other countries could have been in great danger. Only after scientists in Sweden reported radioactive fallout in their country did the Soviets admit that the accident had happened.

In addition, Jews continued to have trouble getting permission to leave Russia. Between 1984 and 1988 only a few thousand were allowed to move to Israel or to some other country.

Perestroika

There was yet another part to the change Mikhail Gorbachev sought to make in the Soviet Union. In a speech he said that "we must restructure ourselves, all of us. I would even say everyone from worker to minister to secretary of the party Central Committee, to the head of the government. Everyone has to master new methods to understand there is no other way for us." This idea was called perestroika.

Many of Russia's problems had to do with the way food, factory goods, and raw materials were produced and sent to where they were needed. Many factory and farm workers did not put in a good day's work. They got paid whether they did their work well or not. Many of the goods factories turned out were of poor quality. Few people in other countries wanted to buy goods made in Russia. But Soviet citizens were eager to buy such goods as recorders, calculators, personal computers, and articles of clothing made in other countries, even though the prices for them were high. Young people would pay more than 200 rubles—over $300—for a pair of jeans made in another nation, for example. Jeans made in Russia were cheaper, but they were of lower quality.

The government had kept the price of food and other goods low. Prices were much lower than what it cost to produce goods and food. Bread was so cheap that some people fed it to chickens and pigs. Apartment rents were so low that they did not pay for the cost of building apartments and keeping them in repair. And there were never enough apartments. People had to wait for years to move into apartments large enough to hold growing families. A person could ride the Moscow subway for only a nickel. But those nickels did not nearly pay the cost of running the subway system. The government made up the difference between what goods cost to produce and what they sold for. This cost billions of rubles a year.

Gorbachev wanted to change all that. He wanted to pay both factory and farm workers for what

Soviet young people seem to long for the glamour of consumer culture and the luxury items such an economy can provide.

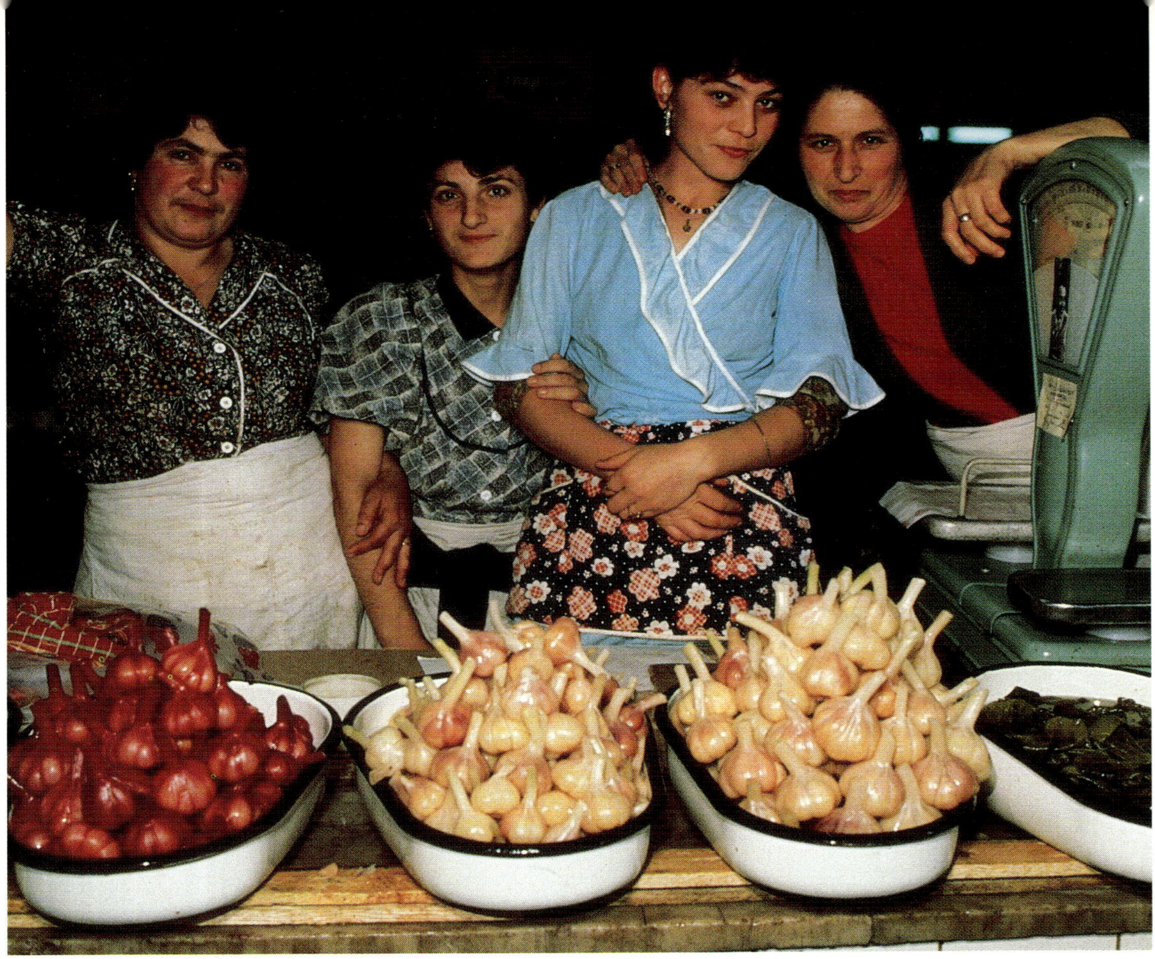

TBS/Reagan

TBS/Reagan

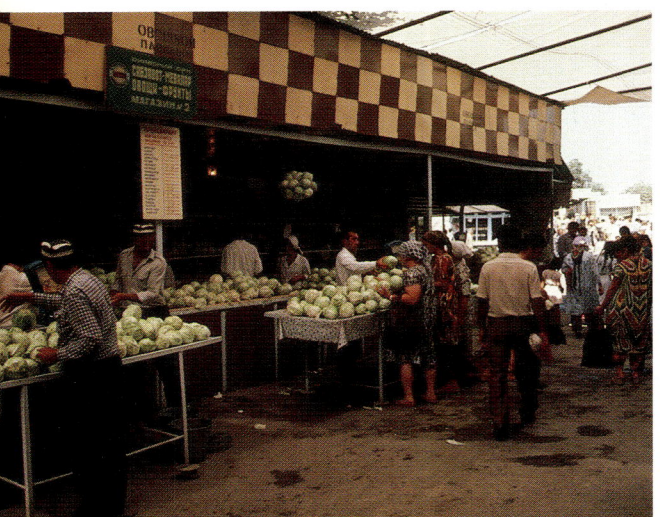

Farmworkers often earn more money from the sale of their own produce than from their jobs on state farms. Shown are market stalls in Moscow (above) *and Samarkand* (left).

they produced. If they did not perform well, their pay would be cut. Gorbachev also wanted the Soviet Union to produce goods of better quality. That would benefit Soviet citizens. It would also give the Soviet Union goods to trade with other nations. In addition, Gorbachev wanted prices to go up enough to pay for the cost of producing goods. He also was in favor of allowing workers to run businesses or do other work in their spare time so they could earn more money.

Farmers on collective farms and state farms did not farm efficiently. This was especially true of farmers who raised grain. The weather was bad in some years, and this held down production. But even in good years, farmers did not grow enough wheat, barley, and corn for the nation. The Soviet Union had to buy grain from other countries. Increasing production on farms would be a difficult problem for the government to solve.

Much of the fruit and vegetables Soviet citizens enjoyed came from small plots of land farmers worked in their spare time. They could sell that food and keep the money they earned. Gorbachev wanted more of that.

Since the Revolution, the government had watched over every part of Soviet life. There grew to be thousands of pages of rules about how much should be produced and where and when, where it should be sent, how much workers should be paid, what prices should be charged for goods, and which people would get which apartments. Writing and carrying out these rules required the labor of hundreds of thousands of government workers. Gorbachev wanted to cut down on rules. That would mean fewer government jobs. Many government workers, from top to bottom, were not enthusiastic about changes perestroika might bring.

Other people in the Soviet Union opposed change because they thought Gorbachev was going against basic ideas of communism. Following his ideas, they thought, could destroy the system. Others did not agree. They believed that Gorbachev aimed to change the system enough to make life in the Soviet Union better for everyone, and to make the nation stronger.

The Soviet Union was still a Communist nation. Government control continued. The secret police were still there, even though they were not as active as during

Mikhail Gorbachev has worked hard to bring his country and the United States closer on important issues such as arms control.

various times in the past. The Soviet Union remained, under communism, a nation with a powerful army, navy, and air force.

The Soviet Union and Other Countries

Under Gorbachev, the Soviet Union continued to aid other nations with Communist governments, such as Cuba, Vietnam, and North Korea, which the United States opposed. But Soviet leaders had second thoughts about the war in Afghanistan.

War there had continued for many years. Thousands of Russian soldiers had been killed or wounded. Still, the Soviet Union could not defeat the rebels who fought the Afghanistan Communist government. In 1987, Gorbachev said that the Soviet Union would gradually remove its troops from Afghanistan. The removal was completed in 1989.

Relations with the United States improved after Mikhail Gorbachev became general secretary. He met five times with President Ronald Reagan in Switzerland, Iceland, Washington, D.C., Moscow, and New York. The main thing they agreed upon was that each side would do away with a certain number of nuclear missiles.

At times, Mikhail Gorbachev spoke of changes he would like to see in the Soviet Union as a "revolution." He did not mean change as great as that which the Russian Revolution had brought in 1917. But he seemed to mean much greater change than the Soviet people had known for many years.

After nearly a decade of fighting, Soviet troops came home from Afghanistan in 1989. Some have compared this war to the experience in Vietnam.

A Chronology of the Soviet Union

800s The Viking Rurik is the first ruler of Russia. The first Russian state is established. Kiev is the center of government.

988 Vladimir I introduces Christianity to Russia. The Cryllic alphabet is adopted.

1200s Russia comes under Mongol rule.

Late 1400s Czar Ivan III ends Mongol rule.

1547 Ivan IV becomes first crowned czar.

1613 After ten years of civil war Michael Romanov becomes czar. His family will rule Russia for three hundred years.

1703 Peter I founds St. Petersburg; he tries to bring Western ways to Russia.

1812 Napoleon invades Russia with an army of 600,000 but is badly defeated.

1825 Some nobles and army officers demand rule by law. Members of this "Decembrist Revolt" are hanged by Nicholas I.

1861 Alexander II frees the serfs. Some towns gain self-government.

1905 Russo-Japanese war is fought, and Russia is defeated. Nicholas II is forced to establish representative government.

1914-1917 With France and England, Russia enters World War I against Germany and Austria-Hungary.

1917 Revolt forces Nicholas I out. Lenin becomes dictator. The Soviet Union withdraws from World War I.

1918-1921 Civil war with anti-Communists rages.

1922 The Union of Soviet Socialist Republics is established.

1924 Lenin dies, and Joseph Stalin gains power over the Communist party.

1929 Stalin becomes dictator.

1939 World War II begins in Europe.

1941 The Soviet Union enters the war on the side of the allies after being attacked by Germany.

Late 1940s In the years following World War II, the Soviet Union takes over Poland, Hungary, Yugoslavia, and other eastern countries, creating the Iron Curtain.

1953 Joseph Stalin dies and Nikita Khrushchev comes to power.

1956 Khrushchev criticizes Stalin's methods of ruling and announces the philosophy of peaceful coexistence with the West.

1957 The Soviet Union launches *Sputnik I*, the first spaceship to orbit the earth.

1960 The Soviet Union brings down a U.S. intelligence-gathering plane.

1961 Yuri Gagarin becomes the first person to orbit the earth.

1962 Soviet missile bases are discovered in Cuba, causing tension between the United States and the Soviet Union. The bases are later removed.

1964 Khrushchev is forced to retire. Leonid Brezhnev becomes head of the Communist party.

1980-1985 Four heads of government die.

1985 Mikhail Gorbachev becomes head of the Communist party. He announces great changes in the Soviet Union in the form of *glasnost* (openness) and *perestroika* (making over).

1985-1988 Gorbachev and President Ronald Reagan meet five times. The Soviet Union and the United States agree to reduce the number of their nuclear weapons.

1989 The Soviet Union withdraws its troops from Afghanistan and also agrees to cut its armed forces by 500,000.

Map of the Soviet Republics

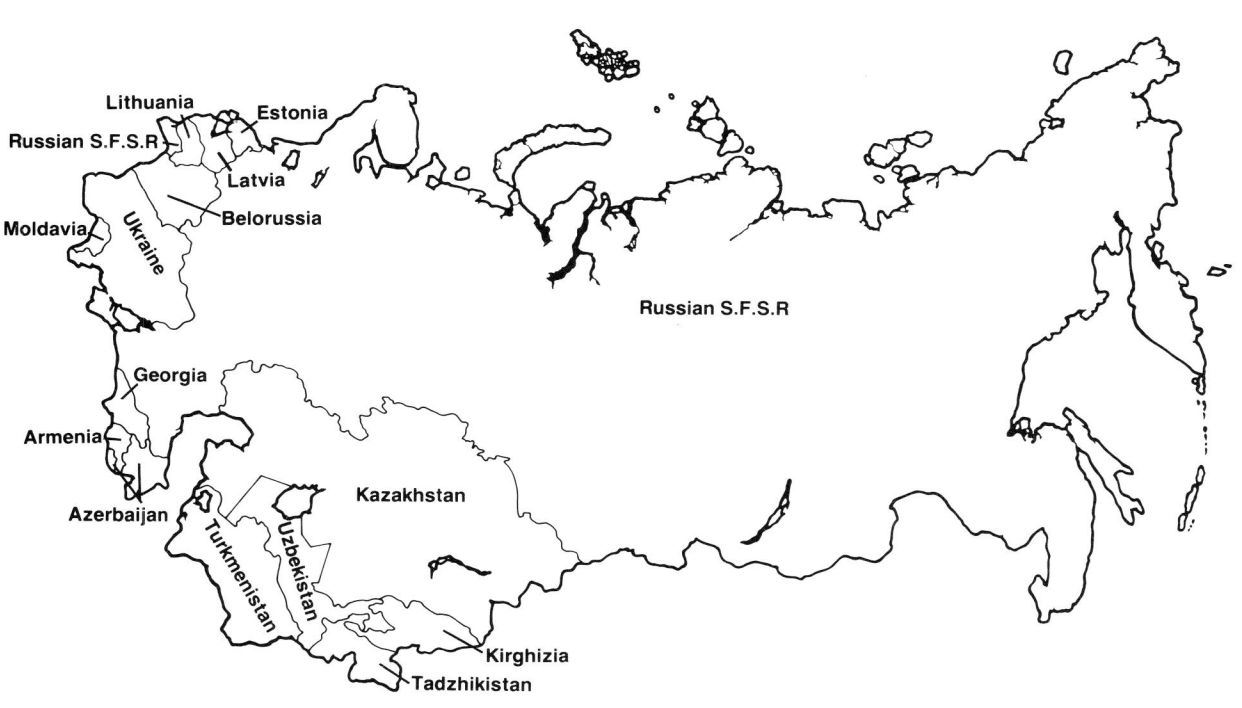

REPUBLIC	POPULATION*	CAPITAL
Russian S.F.S.R.	144,000,000	Moscow
Ukraine	50,900,000	Kiev
Uzbekistan	18,500,000	Tashkent
Kazakhstan	16,000,000	Alma-Ata
Belorussia	10,000,000	Minsk
Azerbaijan	6,700,000	Baku
Georgia	5,270,000	Tbilisi
Tadzhikistan	4,600,000	Dushanbe
Moldavia	4,100,000	Kishinev
Kirghizia	4,000,000	Frunze
Lithuania	3,600,000	Vilnius
Armenia	3,345,000	Erevan
Turkmenistan	3,200,000	Ashkhadbad
Latvia	2,600,000	Riga
Estonia	1,542,000	Tallin

*Mid-1980s estimate

INDEX

Afghanistan, 36, 44-45
Alexander III, 8
Alexandra, 13
apartments, 40

Battle of Stalingrad, 28
Bolsheviks, 11, 12
Brezhnev, Leonid I., 35-36, 36, 37

Carter, Jimmy, 36
Central Committee (of Communist party), 17
Chernobyl, 39
civil war, 13-14
Cold War, 29-31
collective farms, 22, 42
Communist party, 15-17, 24
Communists, 12, 13-14
Congress (of Communist party), 17
Congress of People's Deputies, 14
Council of Ministers, 14-15
Cuba, 33-34

Duma, 6

Eisenhower, Dwight D., 33
Estonia, 13, 26

farm production, 42
Five-Year Plan, 22-23
Five-Year Plan, 25
food, 22, 40
Ford, Gerald, 35
freedoms, individual, 23

Glasnost, 38-39
Gorbachev, Mikhail, 36-38, 39, 40, 42-43, 44, 45
  birth, 37
  education, 37
  relations with citizens, 38
  rise in government, 37
government (structure), 14-17
Great Patriotic War, The, 28

Hitler, Adolf, 25-26
housing, 24
human rights (in Soviet Union), 36

Jews, 31, 36, 39

Kennedy, John F., 34

Khrushchev, Nikita, 32, 33, 34-35

Latvia, 13, 26
Lenin (Vladimir Ilyich Ulyanov), 8-13, 17-18, 21
  becomes dictator, 12
  birth, 8
  exile to Siberia, 10
  family, 8
  flees to Finland, 11
  studies revolution, 8
  tries to seize government, 11
  writings, 10
  youth, 8
Leningrad, 14
Lithuania, 13, 26

medical care, 24
Mensheviks, 11
Moldavia, 26
Moscow, 14

Nicholas II, 6
Nicholas III, 13
Nixon, Richard M., 35
nuclear bomb, 31

Olympic Games (1980), 36
Olympic Games (1984), 36

perestroika, 40-44
Petrograd, 14
Poland, 26
Politburo, 17
premier, 15
Presidium, 14
prices, 40

Reagan, Ronald, 45
Reds, 13
religion, 17
Republic, 14
revolution (1917), 10-12
Romanov (family), 6
Russian Communist Party, 12
Russian Orthodox Church, 17, 21

Sakharov, Andrei, 39
schools, 22-23
Socialist, 14
Soviet of Workers' and Soldiers' Deputies, 10

soviets (councils), 10-11, 14, 17
Soyuz Sovetskikh Sotsialisticheskikh Respublik (S.S.S.R.), 14
Stalin, Joseph (Josif Vissarionovich Djugashvili), 18-21, 22, 24, 26, 29, 30
  becomes dictator, 21
  becomes general secretary of Communist party, 21
  birth, 20
  death, 32
  family, 20-21
  schooling, 21
  sent to Siberia, 21
state farms, 22, 42
subway, 40
Supreme Soviet, 14, 17

"thaw, the," 32-33
Trotsky, Leon, 18, 21

Ulyanov, Alexander, 8
Union, 14
Union of Soviet Socialist Republics (explanation of name), 14

World War I, 6, 10, 11, 13
World War II, 25-28

BRANDYWINE PUBLIC SCHOOLS
Elementary Library
2428 S. 13th Street
Niles, MI 49120